SELF-ENQUIRY

Michael William Bennett

ISBN 1-58898-592-X

SELF-ENQUIRY

We live in an unresolved mystery. It is the mystery of *who* we really are. Who are you? Are you a name? Are you a body? Are you a product of your thought process? Is thought a product of your brain? Is consciousness dependent on thought?

Do you identify yourself as a "soul"? Try to locate the soul. Is it somewhere inside the body? Is the soul an object? Is the soul another word for the mind? Is the "soul" just one more passing thought in a stream of thoughts?

Self-enquiry is the investigation of this mystery. Why investigate? Human nature revolts at its own ignorance. Nothing is more insulting than the absence or loss of identity. As human beings we possess an innate need to investigate. Self-enquiry is what makes us human.

Self-enquiry leads to self-knowledge. Self-enquiry begins by examining our environment. We examine our environment for clues about ourselves. Society is an expression and extension of ourselves. We learn about ourselves by examining society.

———

We live in a world of technology. Technology surrounds us, encapsulates us. We depend on technology every day and can hardly imagine life without it. What is technology? Technology is a means of supplementing survival. Agriculture and simple tool-making are examples of primitive technology. Technology enhances survival. Modern technology, however, has little to do with survival. Most of our technology is devoted to convenience, comfort, pleasure and entertainment.

Modern technology is an extension of our ideological process. It is a manifestation of our values. Where we value pleasure, technology becomes the means of pursuing pleasure. Where we value power over others, technology becomes the means of achieving that power. Technology is not a neutral medium but a means of realizing values. Where technology is firmly established, it becomes a means of enforcing those values. The question is, What are those values?

We are a nation of renters. Even if we own a home, we pay taxes on it. Failure to pay taxes, like failure to pay rent, leads to dispossession. In the city, where population is incredibly dense, many people dwell in apartments, jack-in-the-box homes stacked on top of each other. Others live in the suburbs in gingerbread houses, human display cases that are typically right up alongside each other and close to the road.

If we look in the average home, in the living room, we typically find a television occupying a prominent position. It resembles an idol on the altar of an inner sanctum. Television is one of the most prolific examples of modern technology. People mistakenly regard television as neutral, capable of good or ill depending on the use to which it is put. That is a common mistake made in regard to technology itself.

The very medium of television is fundamentally isolative. Television demands *viewers*, not *participants*. The content on the screen often emphasizes this distinction. Consider violence. When violence is portrayed on television, the viewer merely looks on. The fact that a murder is only *dramatized* escapes the immediate critical notice of the viewer, unless the performance is poorly produced. Television in fact conditions the viewer to respond to perceived violence with quiescence.

There is an ideological process behind television. It is an isolative process that pursues control and dominance. Consider broadcast news. The news is always *telling* us what is going on, what is important, what is *real*. In as much as reality is constructed of information, those who control information shape our reality. They even tell us what the weather is going to do, posturing themselves as the arbiters of Nature Herself. We are constantly told what to think. We are not encouraged to investigate independently, unless to change from one channel to another.

Consider commercial television. Commercials are the most prolific type of broadcast within our culture. Regular television programming is saturated with commercials. Commercials use themes of high impact value, such as sex and violence, to impress their products upon the viewer. The concept of violence includes comparison and competition, aggression, intensity of expression, and a twisting or wrenching of the senses. The violence in commercials is evident in how commercials are directed. There is violence in the angle and jerking of the camera and in the rapid flashing of imagery. Violence often wears the cloak of sarcasm. Commercials typically treat their viewers as simpletons. Commercial interruptions themselves can be considered an act of violence: they violate the flow of a feature presentation.

Commercials typically last less than half a minute. They are purposely short not only to cut the cost of airtime but also to provide a format that demands a highly concentrated content. The purpose of that format is to speedily circumvent the viewer's capacity for analysis. Commercials never allow their viewers the luxury of a lengthy critical examination, despite repetition. Viewers are forced to dizzily swallow commercials like shots of hard liquor.

The news is swallowed as readily as its commercial sponsors, and for similar reasons. The news is typically delivered in a clipped format that does not permit critical analysis. The most prominently featured news stories are those consisting of sex and violence. Sex and violence act as a primer for a message. What is the message? What is the news trying to sell us? Besides commercial products, the news is pitching a paradigm, a perspective of reality. It presents the world as a dangerous place, one that is complex and pricey. Those who live in fear, confusion and debt are easily controlled.

Technology never facilitates relationship. It acts as a buffer or filter between man and the object of relationship. Digital technology is a binary filter through which we quantify the world and others. Through automobiles and airplanes, modern technology has separated people, not drawn them closer together. The telephone, for example, is a symptom of man's separation from man. The telephone only offers the illusion of relationship.

When you talk on the phone you are talking to a machine, not a living being. You are listening to the voice of a machine. The telephone conditions us to regard machine as man. This is dehumanizing. The telephone, particularly the cell phone, often serves as an electronic leash. It is not merely a means of keeping in touch with someone but of keeping tabs on someone. The telephone is a tool for solicitation. Telephone numbers can be compared to tracking devices. Modern technology is a challenge to our right to privacy.

The lure of technology is the promise of individual empowerment. The truth is that technology has become a tool in the hands of authority to exercise greater control over the population. Far from empowering the individual, modern technology has victimized the average man, robbing him of his privacy and forcing him increasingly into a position of dependency.

Technology pretends to expand our options. In fact it limits them. Consider the automobile. It began as a luxury. It became a necessity. Our civilization is automobile-centric. What is an automobile but a box of metal and glass that you sit in for periods of time. Sitting in a box for any length of time is psychologically disturbing. Driving is a monotonous habit of keeping inside the lines and obeying the rules. It is an excellent means of conditioning the public to remain under control.

It is our inalienable right to travel public roads. Traveling by automobile is a privilege, not a right. The automobile is a privilege bestowed on us by technology. It is a privilege we buy into. Urban sprawl, a symptom of automotive technology, makes it difficult to travel in our society without using automotive technology. When the means of supporting oneself is only accessible through automotive technology, that technology has ceased to be a privilege and has become a necessity. The automobile has in fact infringed on our inalienable right to life.

As a pedestrian, do I have an inalienable right to breathe carbon monoxide? Do I possess an inalienable right to an environment damaged by automobiles? Is it my inalienable right to walk beside an endless stream of automotive traffic? I possess the right to life but not a miserable life, not a life of dispossession at the expense of privileging others.

The automobile has subverted our value of distance. Sit in a box, push a pedal and turn a wheel. We measure the "value" of distance at the gas pump. Look at the price of a gallon of gasoline. How *exactly* is that price determined? Notice that it is calculated to the tenth of a cent, as though it were an exact science. Like with income tax, we are led to believe there is an authentically sophisticated basis for calculating the cost. We are led to believe that it obeys some sort of Law like the Pythagorean Theorem or the orbital influence of one of Saturn's moons. The tabulations and explanations amount to nothing more than obfuscation. The truth of the matter is that the basis of the calculation is *greed*.

Money is the subversion of value. What exactly is money? Money is the material medium for quantifying the value of commodities. We quantify the value of commodities for exchange purposes. The nature of that exchange is one of cunning calculation with the intent of turning a profit. Profit is surplus, the sum that remains after expenses are met. Profit is a product of technology. Technology enables us to produce things more easily, faster and in larger quantity. Technology enables us to take advantage of our resources. Money is a form of technology that enables us to take advantage of people. Money becomes a tool for exploiting people.

Frankly, profit is significantly a product of human exploitation. Profit is made when a product is sold for more than its value—value in this case determined by the expense that went into producing the product. Competition in the marketplace may keep prices from soaring beyond the reach of the consumer but this hardly means that prices are equitable. Profit is not excised in competition. Profit, not equitable exchange, is the motive *underlying* competition.

Profit is also made in the workplace where business owners "sell" employment to employees. The less money business owners can get away with paying their employees, the more profit the business owners make. In the workplace human beings have been reduced to a form of technology. Employees are the tools of their employers.

The value of an item in the marketplace is what its owner can get you to pay for it. The value of labor in the workplace is what your employer can get you to agree to. Money is not merely a medium for *quantifying* value. Money *determines* value. Money is a variable, not a constant, and it is manipulated to serve the interests of those who control it.

Retail values reflect the pursuit of profit, not equitable exchange. Retail values are usually calculated to a penny less than a round figure. Retail values bear the semblance of affordability for the sake of sales and profit, not equitable exchange. What, then, is a fair price? Is it merely what the consumer agrees to pay? If someone foolishly agrees to be imprisoned, he is no less of a prisoner than if he is imprisoned by force. Exploitation is most effective when those who are exploited don't even realize they are exploited. If you don't realize you are imprisoned, you won't try to liberate yourself.

Modern civilization denies its citizens independent access to the means of sustenance—that is access to the raw materials for our survival. Such independent access is the cornerstone of material liberty. We are likewise denied education in the skills of sustenance, skills that enable us to derive food, clothing and shelter in the natural world. Modern civilization has substituted the natural world with an artificial one in which the means of sustenance is money. We earn a paycheck. We pay rent. We buy our food at the store. Money is a symbol of labor. Where labor is performed in the absence of genuine liberty, and where that labor is not reimbursed equitably, that labor is another word for slavery. To put it bluntly, money is a symbol of slave labor. Those who possess it in abundance are no better than slave owners, and no more independent than their slaves. Slave owners depend on their slaves.

Regardless of where wage labor is performed, and whether or not the wages are socially respectable, wage labor implies dispossession. The wage laborer is dispossessed. He owns nothing but the wages he earns—money. And money (a symbol, not a commodity) is merely a ticket permitting its possessor to be taken for a ride in the marketplace.

Where there is love, as between family members, each one provides for the other out of mutual affection. Between family members all things are shared in common. There is neither need nor desire to quantify value. Only when human beings define themselves as separate does the need to quantify value arise. Money is a means by which our separative psychology defines itself and pursues its goals. Capital is the sleight of hand by which the few establish dominion over the many. Through money we have replaced brotherly love with bargaining, and genuine equity with comparative shopping.

Poverty is closely related to civilization and the production of wealth. Civilization is typically defined by technological development. Technology involves not only the use of tools but also the efficient use of manpower. The product of technology is not merely sustenance but wealth. Wealth is profit, surplus or excess. It includes convenience, pleasure and entertainment. Advanced technology, in its complexity, necessitates excessive specialization of occupation. Excessive specialization narrows individual capacity and fosters dependency. As a population we have become utterly dependent on technology. We submit to a technological system whose primary purpose is not sustenance but the production of profit—profit for those who command technology. The amount of wealth an individual achieves is determined by his position in relation to technology, more wealth being the result of a greater command or ownership of technology. Our sustenance is also determined by this relationship. The production of sustenance has become so confounded with the production of profit that the two have merged into a single production—money, whose primary purpose remains the production of profit. Poverty is the fate of those who inhabit the foundation of the technological hierarchy, whose relation to technology is one that serves to generate profit rather than accumulate it.

We live in a civilization responsible for maintaining a lower class of labor that is demeaning and dehumanizing. We eat fast food but we don't want to work there. We like computers but we don't want to solder circuit boards on the assembly line. We depend on the trash man but we despise his job.

It is insulting to be told what to do. It is an affront to one's integrity to depend on another for direction rather than to act on one's own behalf. Yet this is precisely the position into which modern technology has forced the average man. In the workplace, knowledge and function have become increasingly compartmentalized. Excessive specialization requires an extensive hierarchical command structure.

Hegemony, manifest in the workplace as the hierarchy of supervision, is an insult to dignity. No one likes to be "under the thumb." People naturally resent being treated like commodities or heads of cattle.

Feudalism has returned in the guise of an information hierarchy. Our democracy is in fact an aristocracy of information and money. We mistakenly regard democracy as egalitarian. In a democracy, people gang up at the expense of the outsider.

We live in a representative democracy. We elect representatives to make our decisions. The larger and more complex our society becomes, the more complicated the issues and the more numerous our representatives. We say we vote our conscience but what we really vote is our ignorance. If a man is knowledgeable enough to make decisions for himself, then why doesn't he make his own decisions? Because in a culture of dependency decisions dictate the actions of others. A "gang" is required to execute those decisions.

Our culture advocates ambition, acquisitive desire, competition, profit, endless technological progress and the worship of creature comforts. These are values that result in dividing society into those who *have* and those who *have not*. These are values that divide society into a hierarchy of dominance in which the few exercise authority over the many. These are values that inevitably lead to violence.

Peace is not the interval between wars. We have only known war. Our society remains at war within its own population continuously. War is waged with weapons that include money and information. People are subjugated even more efficiently through economic and psychological means than through militaristic means. Bloody wars become less frequent as authorities improve their methods of subjugating populations.

There is no honor in war. Murder is the height of disrespect. War is no more just or fair than the value of human life is quantifiable. Bloody war is simply state-sponsored murder. When tax dollars finance the war machine, civilians are just as culpable as those who fire weapons on the front line.

Violence is terrifying, whatever form it takes. The difference between war and terrorism, like the difference between a soldier and a murderer, is merely rhetorical. That sounds harsh but think about it. Terrorism is the use of fear and violence to coerce others. War is simply terrorism on a national scale.

Civilization manifests our values. Society is a projection of our ideological process. What is an ideology? An ideology, whether it is political, economic or religious, is a conceptualization of reality according to which people struggle to conform. When we subscribe to an ideology we strive to become something more than what we are. The psychology of becoming something more than what we are is what I call the paradigm of separation. The paradigm of separation is our most primitive ideology.

According to the paradigm of separation, we identify ourselves as fundamentally separate from one another. Identified as separate, we experience insecurity. We find ourselves in an environment of others over whom we exercise little or no control. This causes us to react with fear. From fear arises a desire for security, a desire for power, position and dominance. We perceive that the only way to be secure is by dominating others. By dominating others we prevent the possibility of being harmed or dominated by them. Others seek to dominate us for similar reasons. The struggle that ensues establishes a social hierarchy consisting of those who occupy positions of authority and those who occupy subservient positions.

We invent ideologies primarily to dominate others, to get people to conform, to make people more predictable and easier to control. Rather than achieving unity or equality, ideologies establish a hierarchy of dominance. That hierarchy is typified in each of its members by the perpetual struggle to become something more than what they are.

Within ideological thinking there is always the division between what we *are* and what we wish to become. Even if a given goal is achieved, it is only achieved according to the internal conditions of its ideology while the psychological paradigm behind the ideology remains. That paradigm is one of intrinsic insecurity, insatiability and division. It makes no difference what the content of the ideology is. Ideologies are always inherently antithetical to genuine cooperation and love.

The paradigm of separation is the blueprint of our civilization. It forms the basis of our politics, our economics, our technology and our culture. The paradigm of separation is the root cause of conflict. Solving this problem is not a question of substituting one ideology for another. The problem is not political, or economic, or technological, but psychological in origin and in solution. We mistakenly identify the symptoms of our problem as the problem itself. In our efforts to resolve the symptoms we fail to address the underlying problem, so the symptoms continually arise despite reform. The problem is not *out there*. The problem is in our own hearts and minds, and that is where we must find the solution.

———

Self-enquiry is unconventional. Self-enquiry does not conform to any organization, ideology or belief. It demands no authority or faith. Self-enquiry is ideally suited for the average person. It is the average person, you and I, who must psychologically transform to end the conflict in ourselves and in the world around us.

Conflict exists throughout our world, undeterred by innovations and undiminished by ideological beliefs. Those in authority—our politicians, our teachers, our employers, the media, and even our so-called moral authorities—have failed to recognize the true cause of conflict, and so have failed to resolve it. Religions offer promises and consolations but no real solution. As a matter of fact, religious belief has often fostered war. Academic philosophy has only taught us clever arguments. It has not resolved conflict.

Conflict is the product of the perspective in which we are born and raised. It is intrinsic to the paradigm that we are conditioned to accept as reality. Conflict is ultimately the result of a psychological process that each of us perpetuates on a daily basis. Conflict does not originate externally. It is the consequence of an internal activity. That activity exists in every human being regardless of race, language, education or geographical location. It is a universal phenomenon generated by *thought*.

We are *always* thinking. Thought is perpetual, continual, incessant. It seems involuntary. Imagine an automobile whose engine is always running, even when the automobile is parked and unused. Our minds are always thinking, even when it is not constructive or functional to do so. This is a clue in our investigation of psychological conflict. It is an indication that something is amiss with the mind.

What are we usually thinking? Most of our thoughts are memories. Our minds are constantly engaged in remembering past events and comparing them with either current situations or imagined possibilities. Our imaginations allow us to remember the past as a sequence of events, thereby enabling us to conceive of the passage of time.

The mind, in thinking, refers to a self upon which all of its memories and experiences are focused. Thoughts revolve around the notion of a thinker. "I" am the thinker. I remember the past and anticipate the future. The thinker recognizes its separation from its environment and from others. The thinker also recognizes the inevitability of death. The recognition of both separation and death creates fundamental insecurity and anxiety. Fear is intrinsic to the separate self and remains for as long as the notion of separation exists.

With the acknowledgment of its separation from others, the thinker also conceives of its separation from its past. In other words, we conceive of the evolution of the self. We imagine that we can become more than what we have been. Thought compares the past with other possibilities and thereby imagines improvements. Thought allows us to recognize our mistakes. It exposes us to the concept of limitation. Everything we have done can be seen as limited by comparison to any number of imagined possibilities. What we have been is never as good as what we *might* have been. What we are is never as good as what we might *become*. This acknowledgment also contributes to our fundamental insecurity. It creates a sense of insufficiency. It inspires us with a *need for fulfillment*. It is our motivation to improve ourselves, to become more than what we perceive ourselves to be, to progress toward any number of imagined goals.

We perceive ourselves as separate from others, separate from our environment, even separate from ourselves in as much as we can project an idea or ideal of ourselves into the future. We remain profoundly insecure and anxious. From this anxiety arise innumerable desires for security, for comfort and for safety. We desire control over our environment to ensure our survival and the fulfillment of our goals. Ideally, we seek to replace the natural world with an artificial one of our own engineering over which we can exercise complete control. Through industry and technology we have virtually accomplished this. We desire to dominate and control others since others pose a potential threat to our security. In this way we tend to regard others as objects for manipulation rather than as individuals. In the hierarchy of dominance that is human society today, we have essentially locked human beings into positions in an artificial system wherein their movements are limited and predictable.

The chronic thought process generates a separative perspective in which we recognize ourselves as separate beings that are conditioned, limited and unfulfilled. We seek fulfillment through the acquisition of possessions. We seek fulfillment through the experience of pleasure. We seek an escape from our perennially craven condition through an endless variety of sensual and intellectual entertainments. We spend enormous amounts of our time and energy manufacturing things through which we seek fulfillment. We claim these things enhance life. The shopping malls are full of them. They are symptoms of our psychological dilemma.

From the perspective of the separate self, life is an endless contest for dominance, an endless struggle for self-improvement, an endless pursuit of pleasure. It is anxiety and fear, cravenness and desire, conflict and sorrow. As long as we live from the separative perspective, we are bound to experience conflict—conflict within ourselves between who we think we are and who we wish to become, conflict between each other and conflict between ourselves and Nature. This is the origin of sorrow. Everyone associates sorrow with the ending of a pleasure, or with their lack of a possession, or with their relative position to others, rather than to the perspective itself that motivates them.

Desires arise as a response to the fear that is intrinsic to the separate self. Desire is a symptom of separation. The pursuit of *any* desire reinforces separation and therefore perpetuates conflict. When I recognize that a *particular* desire of mine leads to conflict, I may relinquish that desire. By relinquishing a desire, my sensitivity increases. Most people cannot bear to be sensitive to their everyday craven condition, so they eagerly pursue any number of desires and distractions. Only someone who thoroughly recognizes the utter futility of a desire will relinquish that desire. This comes about by observing the origin and consequence of the desire. Real detachment is not an effort to divorce oneself from something. Real detachment is an easy release of what is recognized as unnecessary or self-destructive.

By relinquishing the pursuit of desires that lead to obvious forms of conflict, we acquire greater energy and awareness. Here is an important clue in our investigation. Energy and awareness are closely related. Wherever I direct my awareness, my energy is there. Likewise, where I direct my energy my awareness is there. Energy and awareness are really aspects of one phenomenon. I call it the Force of consciousness.

The Force is the very medium of sensation and perception. It is like an electromagnetic energy that can be experienced throughout the body. It is awareness whose center of identification is not fixed but is fluid. The Force is the movement of consciousness toward its source. The Force *is* self-enquiry.

The choice to relinquish any desire is made by the one who chooses, the thinker, the center of our identification as separate beings. Choice is a movement from a center of identification. That center is itself the separative perspective. Any desire to relinquish desire is itself a desire and therefore perpetuates desire.

Precisely *who* am I? This is the essence of self-enquiry. Am I the thinker? Am I the separate self? We identified ourselves within the paradigm of separation, pursuing desires, struggling for dominance and experiencing conflict. When we begin to relinquish the pursuit of desires we acquire more energy and awareness. Detachment leads to the perception of the Force. The contraction of the Force is experienced as tension or stress in various areas of the body that correspond to various aspects of life.

The contraction of the Force is our identification as the separate self. The contraction is relinquished when we no longer identify ourselves as separate. The more we release the Force from contraction, the more we become aware of ourselves *as* the Force of consciousness. The Force begins to circulate, rising toward the top of the head. The Force ascends from the gross to the subtle. As the Force of consciousness increases, so does our intuition of *who* we really *are*.

Right conduct facilitates self-enquiry. Right conduct is not a model for behavior or a code of conduct to conform to. Conformity, conditioning and coercion reinforce the paradigm of separation. Right conduct is whatever is expedient to circulate the Force. Right conduct is simply what facilitates self-enquiry in every area of life. Moderation is the key to right conduct.

Chronic conceptual thought will attempt to hijack a physiological drive, such as hunger or sexuality, in order to perpetuate its separative agenda. Chronic conceptual thought will exacerbate a physiological drive for the purpose of contracting the Force. Energy is dissipated in this activity, giving the psychologically craven perspective a form of release or escape. This "escape" is really only a trap.

A lie is made convincing by association with a truth. The agenda of chronic conceptual thought is to convince you that by indulging in a genuine physiological drive you will fulfill your psychological cravenness. The truth is the physiological drive. The illusion is your psychological cravenness. Learn to disassociate the lie from the truth, and observe right conduct.

Energy gathers naturally. Life is a movement of energy. What we do with that energy determines our condition. If we misidentify ourselves as separate, then we dissipate energy. That dissipation of energy leads to sorrow. If we stop pushing against the current of life, if we simply let the Force take its natural course, then we allow the circuit of energy to complete itself. We establish integrity.

Sorrow is the result of our false identification. The separate self is a product of conceptual thought. Conceptual thought is the capacity to compare memories and draw associations between them. The associations we draw between them are concepts. A concept may be defined as the assumption of similarity or identity between different things. We only *conceive* of similarities. Our sensory impressions are fundamentally dissimilar and different. For example, the concept of Table identifies any number of distinctly different objects. One table has four corners, another is round. One table has four legs and another has only one. Tables that *appear* the same are different under closer examination. Even if they appear the same they remain distinctly different objects. And any given table does not *remain* the same through time since everything changes from moment to moment. It is a tacit contradiction to equate two different things. Conceptual thought appears to be founded on this contradiction.

We commit conceptual contradiction because it is *useful* to do so. It is an extension of our instinct to survive. Conceptual thought reflects the characteristic of our survival instinct to conserve energy. By conceiving of similarities between objects, and assuming consistencies through the passage of time, we can use our energy to greater advantage for our survival.

Concepts begin simply as combinations of impressions of our five senses. As concepts become more prolific they become more complex. We invent symbols that we associate with our impressions in order to more easily organize them. We conceive of language to facilitate communication. Conceptual thought creates its own perspective of reality. Through conceptual thought we perceive ourselves as separate from others. Just as we conceive of objects remaining consistent through time, we conceive of ourselves as thinkers who remain consistent through time. The thinker itself is a concept. From the perspective of the thinker, experience *is* conceptual. The thinker has no more relationship with "reality" than any other concept. Everything the thinker perceives is conceptual. My conception of a particular table, for instance, is what I call a "concrete concept." As a thinker, when I look at that table I am actually perceiving a "concrete concept" of that table. The notion that the table exists independent of conceptualization is itself a concept. "I" only perceive concepts. My conception of tables in general is what I call an "abstract concept." That "abstract concept" is itself defined in terms of other concepts. Concepts define one another.

Complex concepts are defined by simpler concepts that are in turn defined by even simpler concepts, until the definition is ultimately resolved into a set of irreducible ideas defined in relation to one another. Ideas *only* possess meaning *in relation* to one another.

For example, any given quantity is defined by the concept of Quantity itself. The concept of Quantity is defined by the concepts of the Singular (that is, one) and the Multiple (two or more). The concept of the Singular is comprehensible only in relation to the concept of the Multiple, and vice versa. A Multiple *consists* of Singulars, and a Singular only exists *in contrast* to Multiples.

Opposites define one another. In other words, they are defined by what they are *not*. Any idea or concept defined in its annihilation has no meaning *in itself*. A meaning that can only be understood in reference to its contradiction is in itself meaningless. It exists, but only as a mirage exists—our belief in what it signifies is an illusion.

What is self-evident, by definition, requires no reference external to itself. What is self-evident is absolutely certain, independently complete. The question of self-evidence is the question of *identity*. It is the question of self-enquiry. Who, or what, am I?

I experience a steady stream of sensory impressions of myself. I feel my heartbeat, for example. What is sensory awareness? The "sensation" of my heartbeat is ultimately registered in my brain where I actually "perceive" it. In other words, what seems to be taking place in my chest is actually taking place in my brain. Sensory awareness can be understood as an activity occurring in the brain.

Conceptual thought is an activity of the brain. "My heartbeat" is a concept. "My heartbeat" does not exist independent of the brain. The notion that "my heartbeat" exists independent of the brain is itself a concept, a product of the activity of the brain. Only the brain and its activity can be said (with any certainty) to "exist." But the "brain" is also a concept. The "brain" does not exist independent of conceptual thought. The notion that the "brain" exists independent of conceptual thought is itself a concept. Conceptual thought is the only activity that can be said (with any certainty) to exist.

My perceptions, sensory and psychological, are reducible to the content of conceptual thought.

A concept identifies any particular "material" thing (such as my body) by contrasting it with other "material" things (such as the space surrounding it, and other bodies). No concept is independently complete. My concept of any "material" thing is based on the *assumption* that the "material" thing remains consistent through time. For instance, I assume that my "body" is the same body *now* as it was when I began this sentence, despite the fact that my *perception* of it has "materially" *changed*. In fact, my "body" is *different*. Concepts that identify a multitude of things (such as bodies in general) do so by (conceptually) *identifying* distinctly *different* things (different bodies). Far from being self-evident, conceptual thought is founded on assumption and contradiction.

While the content of conceptual thought is in a state of constant flux and contradiction, "I" seem to remain consistent. *Who* am I? "I" am a concept, a reference to an originator of conceptual thought. The concept of "self" is merely another concept. It is not itself original. The concept of "self" is dependent on the conceptual thought process. It is not self-evident.

If "I" am merely another concept, another aspect of the ever changing and contradictory content of conceptual thought, then can the *activity* of conceptual thought itself be considered self-evident? The conceptual thought process seems perpetual. Everything we perceive and know depends upon it. Even our concept of "self" is a product of conceptual thought. This very investigation utilizes conceptual thought. But thinking is only evident when there is an *awareness* of it taking place.

Is awareness a product of conceptual thought? We are typically only "aware" of thought. What *is* awareness? If one becomes aware of the *activity* of thought rather than the *content* of thought, the thought process begins to "slow down." The sequence of one thought leading to the next becomes clarified. Through persistent observation—not concentrating but by *paying attention*—the conceptual thought process is eventually recognized as a *voluntary process*. A voluntary process can be voluntarily relinquished.

———

Consciousness itself is non-conceptual. *Who* we really are is self-evident.

The Self is universal. It is without separation. It is a Microcosm, a perfectly proportioned totality. It is the epitome of Beauty.

Knowledge of Self is not separate from Self. The two are identical. Self-knowledge is not derived from outside of ourselves. We cannot *acquire* an authentic identity.